Discussing Mere Christianity

Discussing Mere Christianity

Exploring the History, Meaning, & Relevance *of* C. S. Lewis's Greatest Book

Study Guide
Eight Sessions

Written by
Devin Brown

ZONDERVAN®

ZONDERVAN

Discussing Mere Christianity Study Guide

This title is also available as a Zondervan ebook. Visit www.zondervan.com/ebooks.

Requests for information should be addressed to:
Zondervan, *3900 Sparks Dr. SE, Grand Rapids, Michigan 49546*

ISBN 978-0-310-69984-2

Cover design: Ron Huizinga
Cover photography: Used by permission of The Marion E. Wade Center, Wheaton College, Wheaton, Illinois
Interior design: Dan Dingman

First Printing April 2015 / Printed in the United States of America

CONTENTS

How to Use This Study Guide

This study guide is not meant to replace reading *Mere Christianity* by C. S. Lewis. Its purpose is to give you a better understanding of and a greater appreciation for Lewis's beloved classic. For each of the eight sessions, there will be a reading assignment. Be sure to read the assigned chapters from *Mere Christianity* first and then work through the commentary and discussion questions. You will also find a number of quotations taken from other books Lewis wrote. To make the reading easier, page numbers (noted in parentheses) are given only for quotations from *Mere Christianity.*

This study guide has been designed to accompany the eight-session video, *Discussing Mere Christianity.* Each of the video sessions is hosted by Eric Metaxas and features teaching from a variety of well-known Lewis scholars and readers, as well as comments from two people who met Lewis when he was alive: Walter Hooper, who was Lewis's secretary and then became the literary executor of the C. S. Lewis estate, and Douglas Gresham, Lewis's stepson.

There are two ways to use this study guide. If you are **leading a group**, first watch the video together—each session's presentation is approximately 20 minutes long. Then, depending on how much time you have, select one or more of the questions provided for discussion. You may use the commentary sections however you like during the group gathering—read them aloud, read them silently, summarize them, read specific portions, or read none at all, saving them for a later time. You may also want to read aloud one or more of the relevant passages from *Mere Christianity.*

If you are studying *Mere Christianity* **as an individual**, first complete the reading assignment and then work through each chapter in the study guide, writing out your responses to the questions in the space provided. (You may still use the video, of course!)

There is also a section for **Personal Study** at the conclusion of each session. This is designed for you to dig a little deeper into questions raised from the book that will enhance your reading experience of *Mere Christianity.*

Finally, with a limit of eight sessions designed to fit within the time constraints of a Sunday school class or book club, this study guide does not cover all of *Mere Christianity.* Hopefully after finishing these eight sessions, you will go on to read C. S. Lewis's greatest book in its entirety.

It All Began with a Letter

On a frosty February morning in 1941, as England began another year of fighting in the war against Germany, C. S. Lewis turned to the stack of mail on his desk and noticed a letter from a correspondent whose name was unfamiliar to him.

"Dear Mr. Lewis," the writer began, "I address you by name because, although we have never met, you cannot be a stranger after allowing me—and many others—to know some of your thoughts and convictions in your book *The Problem of Pain*."

The letter was from James Welch, the Director of Religious Broadcasting for the BBC. What no one at the time could have guessed—not Welch, Lewis, or anyone else—was that this letter would usher in a major turning point in Christian apologetics and would be the pivot around which Lewis's tremendous Christian output would swing.

For the previous fifteen years of his life, Lewis had been a fellow at Oxford's Magdalen College. At this point, he had published two very early books of poetry. Then, after becoming a Christian in 1931, he had published *The Pilgrim's Regress* (1933), an allegory tracing his own journey to the Christian faith, and *The Problem of Pain* (1940), which explored the question of how a good and all-powerful God could create a world with evil and suffering. Adding to these, partly on the prompting of his good friend, J. R. R. Tolkien, Lewis had written a science fiction novel titled *Out of the Silent Planet* (1938), the story of a Cambridge linguist who was kidnapped and taken to Mars where he became caught up in interplanetary spiritual warfare.

While this output was significant, Welch's use of the term *many others* in referring to the readers of *The Problem of Pain* was a relatively modest use of the phrase, referring to thousands of readers, not the millions that Lewis's books would later have.

"I write to ask whether you would be willing to help us in our work of religious broadcasting," Welch continued. "The microphone is a limiting, and rather irritating, instrument, but the quality of thinking and depth of conviction which I find in your book ought sure to be shared with a great many other people."

Welch suggested two possible topics. The first was for Lewis to speak about the Christian assumptions, or the lack of Christian assumptions, that underlie modern literature. The other topic Welch proposed was a series of talks loosely titled "The Christian Faith as I See It—by a Layman."

Lewis wrote back to thank Welch for his kind remarks. Noting that the first topic about modern literature did not suit him, Lewis agreed to try his hand at the second.

Six months later—on Wednesday, August 6, 1941—Lewis boarded the train for the hour-long trip from Oxford to London. He then traveled on to the BBC's Broadcast House for the first in the series of five talks. Each week, at precisely 7:45 in the evening, the "On the Air" light would blink on, and Lewis would spend the next fifteen minutes speaking to a weary and war-torn nation about such topics as moral law and humanity's relationship to one higher than itself.

To the surprise of everyone, including Lewis himself, the talks were a huge success. Lewis's clear, step-by-step reasoning, his honest and unassuming tone, and his use of commonsense examples drew in listeners of all types. The BBC invited Lewis to present a second series of talks several months later, and then a third the following year, and finally a fourth series in 1944. The talks were originally published as separate works. Then, in 1952, they were collected into one volume and published as the book the world today knows as *Mere Christianity.* Many claim it is Lewis's greatest book.

Today, *Mere Christianity* appears on virtually every list of the most influential Christian books of the twentieth century. A long list of new converts point to it as an indispensable element in their conversion. An equally long list of mature Christians cite it as having been an essential part of their Christian growth and discipleship.

And it all began with a letter.

Devin Brown is a Lilly Scholar and a professor of English at Asbury University where he teaches a class on C. S. Lewis.

1

Our Sense of Right and Wrong

Reading Assignment

In preparation for Session 1, read the following from *Mere Christianity*:

- ◊ The Preface
- ◊ Book 1, Chapter 1: "The Law of Human Nature"
- ◊ Book 1, Chapter 2: "Some Objections"

Watch Video: *Our Sense of Right and Wrong*

Play the video segment for Session 1. As you watch, take any notes that might be helpful to you, using the space provided below.

Notes

Video Discussion

As Eric Metaxas explains in the video, *Mere Christianity* was written because James Welch happened to read one of C. S. Lewis's books and decided to write him a letter with a surprising invitation. What about you? Have you experienced an event in your life which may have seemed coincidental at the time but later felt as though the hand of God was behind it? Maybe just the right book came to you at just the right time. Maybe a job opened up right when you needed one. Maybe you just happened to meet someone who went on to play a key role in your life.

Question 1. The poet William Cowper wrote, "God works in mysterious ways, his wonders to perform." Describe a time when God worked in a mysterious way in your life. How did you know only God could have orchestrated it?

Lewis's Preface to *Mere Christianity*

Near the start of the Preface, Lewis lays out the central approach he will take for the rest of the book. He tells us that his purpose is *not* to offer help to readers who are trying to decide which Christian denomination to join. "You will not learn from me whether you ought to become an Anglican, a Methodist, a Presbyterian, or a Roman Catholic," he writes (viii). Instead, Lewis's goal is to explain and defend what he calls *mere* Christianity, the core beliefs shared by all Christians at all times.

Lewis goes on to claim that discussions—we might say battles—about the denominational issues that divide Christians are more likely to deter outsiders than bring them into the fold. With the rise of ecumenism, it may be hard for us to understand just how radical *Mere Christianity* was in its time. It wasn't uncommon for each Christian denomination to promote its own distinctives and superiority over other denominations. Lewis sidestepped that approach, choosing instead to write about the most common and unifying Christian beliefs. This is also remarkable when we consider that Lewis was born and raised in Belfast, Northern Ireland, where the conflict between the Protestants and Catholics was especially intense.

Question 2. Discuss one or more of the following:

- Describe one or more of the specific issues that Christians often fight about.
- Do you agree with Lewis that when talking with non-Christians it is better to focus on those things all Christians believe? Why or why not?
- Why do you think many Christians focus their energies on what divides believers rather than on what unites them?

Book 1, Chapter 1: The Law of Human Nature

Everyone has heard people quarreling.

These are the very first words that went out over the air in Lewis's first BBC talk, as well as the opening words to chapter one of *Mere Christianity.* Rather than beginning with a discussion of the doctrines of Christianity—complex topics such as sin, atonement, salvation, the deity of Christ, or the Trinity—Lewis begins with a subject that people all over the world, believers or not, can relate to.

Everyone has heard people quarreling.

Lewis opens chapter one, "The Law of Human Nature," by describing how when one person tries to convince another that they should or should not have done something, he is not merely saying that the second person's behavior did not happen to please him. Instead the first person is saying that there is a standard of right and wrong behavior which the second person has violated—and the first person expects the second to know about and accept this standard.

The accused person, in turn, makes the case that he or she has *not* done anything wrong, or that there was justification or extenuating circumstances in committing this wrong. Lewis's point is that there would be no reason to try to do this *unless both people have a shared understanding of what right and wrong are.* Quarreling between two people suggests that there is some kind of objective right and wrong that exists beyond our own personal wants and wishes. Lewis calls this sense of right and wrong "The Law of Human Nature."

Question 3. Lewis claims that disputes between people mean there must be a higher authority to whom they are appealing. Do you find his argument convincing? Why or why not?

Lewis himself had many colleagues at Oxford who claimed to be *moral relativists*, people who believed that the standards of right and wrong were simply rules society had made up—like the law about which side of the road people are supposed to drive on. Toward the end of chapter one, Lewis comments that whenever we find someone who says he does not believe in a real right and wrong, we find the same person going back on this a moment later. As soon as this person thinks someone else has done him wrong, he complains about it as though there was a real external standard by which actions ought to be judged.

Tim Keller, who was greatly influenced by the writings of C. S. Lewis, addresses this issue in his book *The Reason for God*. Keller writes:

> Conservative writers and speakers are constantly complaining that the young people of our culture are relativistic and amoral. As a pastor in Manhattan I have been neck-deep in sophisticated twentysomethings for almost two decades, and I have not found this to be the case. The secular, young adults I have known have a very finely honed sense of right and wrong. There are many things happening in the world that evoke their moral outrage. There is a problem with their moral outlook, however.

These young people whom Keller describes *claim* to believe that all moral values are relative and that one person should not impose his or her values on someone else. At the same time they also believe that there is a moral standard by which all people should abide. For example, they might view crimes like rape and genocide as absolute wrongs for everyone everywhere, whether or not other people from other cultures agree or not.

Question 4. In the video, Alister McGrath refers to those who believe that morality is "just about me doing what I think is right." Briefly describe what someone who believes right and wrong are personal preferences might say to someone who, like Lewis, claimed there is a real standard of right and wrong. Does this person live according to their beliefs? If not, where is the contradiction?

Book 1, Chapter 2: Some Objections

In a letter to his friend Arthur Greeves, Lewis commented, "One gets funny letters after broadcasting—some from lunatics who sign themselves 'Jehovah' or begin 'Dear Mr. Lewis, I was married at the age of 20 to a man I didn't love'—but many from serious inquirers whom it was a duty to answer fully."

Here in chapter two, Lewis replies to objections he had received. One of these objections was to his claim that there is a moral absolute. The listeners asserted that all morality is merely a *social convention* which "human beings have made up for themselves and might have made different if they had liked" (12). As evidence for this claim, Lewis's objectors pointed to the fact that there have been differences between the moral ideas of one time and another time or between one country and another.

Lewis reminds readers that when there are differences, these differences are not nearly as great as his objectors imagined. And when we find discernable differences between cultures, Lewis observed, we all agree that some moralities are better than others. In fact, if it was not possible for one set of moral ideas to be better or truer than any other, Lewis argues, then there would be "no sense in preferring civilized morality to savage morality or Christian morality to Nazi morality" (13). And, of course, as soon as we say that one set of moral values can be seen as better than another, we are actually measuring both sets by an independent standard and saying one set conforms more nearly to that standard than the other. Moral ideas, however, are different from social conventions.

Social conventions are the rules a society creates for itself to accommodate specific needs and demands. One example already mentioned is driving on the left side of the road—a perfect illustration, since in many parts of the world people are taught to drive on the right side. Another example of a social convention is how we greet our friends. In some places people shake hands. In others they may hug, bow, kiss one another on the cheek, or not touch each other at all. While we can easily conceive of how driving on the opposite side of the road would be perfectly acceptable, we find it very hard to conceive of how murder or theft could be viewed as being good instead of evil.

Question 5. In the video, Alister McGrath says that *right* is not something that we humans invent or arbitrate—it is already there. Can you think of more examples which illustrate the difference between moral absolutes and social conventions?

To avoid the charge that Lewis is misrepresenting those who believe that all morality is subjective, here it might be helpful to allow a secular philosopher to speak for himself. In an essay titled "Science and Ethics," Bertrand Russell puts forth his belief that all moral values are subjective. Russell writes:

> The theory which I have been advocating is a form of the doctrine which is called the "subjectivity" of values. This doctrine consists in maintaining that, if two men differ about values, there is not a disagreement as to any kind of truth, but a difference of taste. If one man says "oysters are good" and another says "*I* think they are bad," we recognize that there is nothing to argue about. The theory in question holds that all differences as to values are of this sort ... The difference is one of tastes, not one as to any objective truth.
>
> The consequences of this doctrine are considerable. In the first place, there can be no such thing as "sin" in any absolute sense; what one man calls "sin" another may call "virtue."

Most people have heard a version of the argument Russell makes here—that what one person may see as good, another person may see as bad, and so there can be no such thing as objective or universal moral values.

At the end of chapter two, Lewis comes to the opposite conclusion. Lewis maintains that though differences between people's ideas of what constitutes decent behavior might make us suspect there no is real natural law of behavior, the things we think about these differences "really prove just the opposite" (14). Lewis points to the differences between the English moral principles and those of the Nazis. No one listening to his radio broadcast would have said, "What was right for the Nazis was right for them. Who are we to say that their exterminating the Jews or their invading another sovereign country is wrong?"

Question 6. Can you point to an example in today's world of a culture or group of people with a radically different view of what is accepted as decent behavior? Does this difference mean there is no real right or wrong?

Individual Activity: What I Want to Remember

Complete this activity on your own.

◊ Briefly review the readings and any notes you took.

◊ In the space below, write down the most significant thing you gained in this session—from your reading, video content, or discussion material.

What I want to remember from this session . . .

Closing Prayer

Close your time together in prayer.

Session 1 Personal Study

Reflect further by exploring additional material from *Mere Christianity* and Scripture.

At the end of the Preface of *Mere Christianity*, Lewis presents a now famous image where he describes mere Christianity as a large hallway in a house and the various denominations of Christianity as the rooms that branch off this hall. Lewis's hope, he tells us, is to help people come to believe these central beliefs shared by all Christians, to help bring them into the hall. But the journey is not meant to end in the hallway; it is meant to continue on to a specific church. The hall, Lewis explains, is a place to wait in, where a person can "try the various doors"—not a place where anyone should permanently live (xv).

Lewis was critical of the church-shopping which took place in his day (and continues today). In deciding which door to go through, which church to attend, he urges readers not to focus on the "paint and paneling" or any of the external aspects (xvi), but on whether the doctrines are true and if there is an emphasis on holiness. As is fitting, given his focus on the shared beliefs that unite all Christians, Lewis ends the Preface with a plea for compassion, as he calls for his readers to "be kind to those who have chosen different doors" (xvi).

In the six decades since Lewis first came up with his image of the hallway of the house with many rooms branching off, there has—in parts of the world—been an increased emphasis on the beliefs that unite all Christians and a rise in nondenominational congregations.

Question 1. Do you agree with Lewis that the mere Christianity of the hallway is not a place where Christians should live? Does Lewis's image still fit? Why or why not?

In the very first pages of *Mere Christianity*, Lewis establishes the approach he will use for the entire book. He does not ask us to shut down our minds and simply accept something by faith. Nor does he ask us to believe merely because we feel it is right. Instead of asking us to think less, Lewis actually pushes us to think more than we normally do, to think more carefully, more deeply, and with less prejudice than we may have in the past. In a later chapter, titled "Faith," Lewis states, "I am not asking anyone to accept Christianity if his best reasoning tells him that the weight of the evidence is against it" (140). Throughout *Mere Christianity* Lewis invites us to use not just our reason but our best reasoning.

Question 2. Why do you think some Christians are reluctant to use their minds when it comes to faith? Why are various people of faith opposed to or suspicious of reason?

Question 3. This session explored the idea that humans have an inner sense of right and wrong which Lewis refers to as the Law of Human Nature. What does the following passage from Romans say about our inner sense of right and wrong? Can you think of other Scripture passages that might also be relevant?

> *Indeed, when Gentiles, who do not have the law, do by nature things required by the law, they are a law for themselves, even though they do not have the law. They show that the requirements of the law are written on their hearts, their consciences also bearing witness, and their thoughts sometimes accusing them and at other times even defending them.*
>
> Romans 2:14–15

Reading Assignment

In preparation for Session 2, read the following from *Mere Christianity*:

- ◊ Book 1, Chapter 4: "What Lies Behind the Law"
- ◊ Book 1, Chapter 5: "We Have Cause to Be Uneasy"

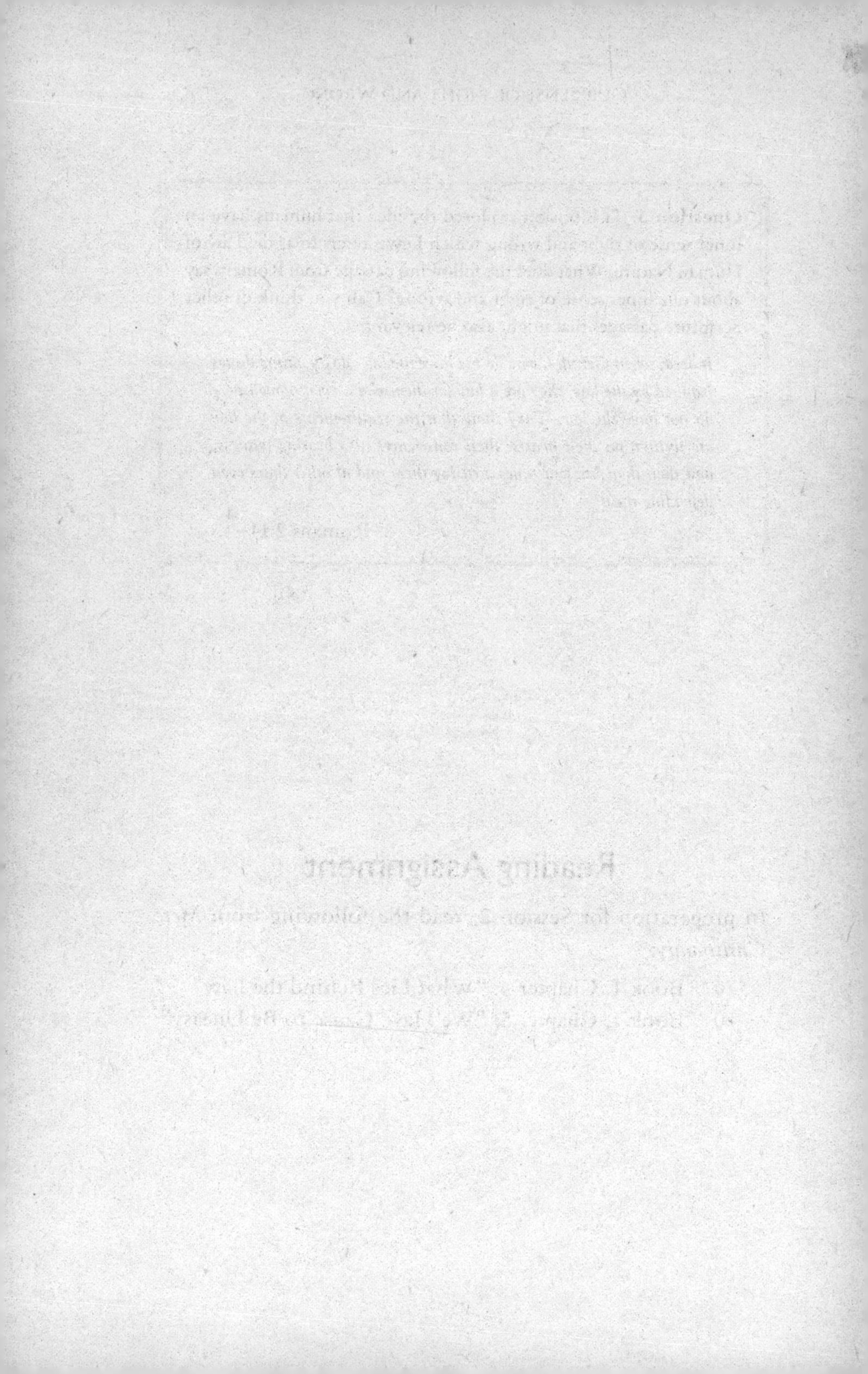

2

What's Behind Our Sense of Right and Wrong

Reading Assignment

In preparation for Session 2, read the following from *Mere Christianity*:

- ◊ Book 1, Chapter 4: "What Lies Behind the Law"
- ◊ Book 1, Chapter 5: "We Have Cause to Be Uneasy"

Watch Video: *What's Behind Our Sense of Right and Wrong*

Play the video segment for Session 2. As you watch, take any notes that might be helpful to you in the space provided.

Notes

Video Discussion

Book 1, Chapter 4: What Lies Behind the Law

In the first three chapters, Lewis made the case that there really is an objective law of right and wrong, a set of moral principles that society did not create, which becomes clear when people quarrel. Here in chapter four Lewis now turns to what might be behind this law. In the second paragraph, Lewis points out that ever since humans have been able to think, they have wondered what the universe really is and how it came to be. He then goes on to describe the two general views which humans have taken on this subject.

Question 1. In the video, Jerry Root talks about the two ways to look at the world which Lewis presents in chapter four—the materialist view and the religious, or supernatural, view. Can you briefly sum up these two views of the universe? Do you know of anyone who takes the materialist view, or has there been a point in your life when this was your own view? Can you think of any implications that having the materialist view would have on how someone lives life?

Having explained the two general views of the universe, Lewis comments that we cannot find out which view is the correct one by science in the ordinary sense. He first makes it clear that he is not anti-science. Science has a very important and very necessary job to do as it conducts experiments, observes, and reports on the physical universe. But according to Lewis, the scientific method cannot answer every question, including whether or not there is something *beyond* the physical universe. Science cannot say whether the materialist view or the religious view is correct. Lewis concludes that if there is something behind the things science can observe, then it "will have to remain altogether unknown to men or else make itself known in some different way" (23).

According to Lewis, when science goes beyond making statements about the physical world, it is no longer making scientific statements and at that point is no longer science but what he refers to in other places as *scientism*.

Question 2. In the video, Jerry Root claims that our world is far too complex to be reduced merely to the quantifiable and measurable. Do you agree, and if so, why?

Near the end of chapter four, Lewis stops to remind readers that he is "not yet within a hundred miles" of the God found in Christianity (25). Having first begun with the image of two people quarreling about whether or not one of them has done anything wrong, Lewis then goes on to suggest that we all have a universal sense of right and wrong, and at the same time we also have a sense that we are not keeping this law of right and wrong.

So where are we at this point? Lewis reports: "All I have got to is a Something which is directing the universe, and which appears in me as a law urging me to do right and making me feel responsible and uncomfortable when I do wrong" (25). Then he tells us that in the next chapter, we will see if we can find anything more about this Something.

In the first four chapters, Lewis has had two general points he wanted to make. First, people all over the world have a curious idea that humans should behave in a certain way—in the video, Jerry Root refers to this as insider information. Second, people know that they do not live up to this standard of behavior—they do not always behave the way they feel they ought. And in this second point Lewis makes it clear that he includes himself.

Question 3. As Jerry Root explains in the video, Lewis is not standing off to the side suggesting he is flawless and condemning all the sins and shortcomings of those who are not as morally perfect as he is. Lewis makes it clear that his approach is simply that of one sinner talking to another because we all fail to live up to the moral law within us. Why is this approach more effective? Why is this approach often hard for some Christians to accept?

Question 4. Understanding that we all have a sense of right and wrong and that there must be something or *someone* real behind the universal experience was a pivotal first step for Lewis. Lewis realized that he could not even live up to the standards he set for himself. Why might the God of grace who makes available forgiveness and loves people in spite of what they do provide a newfound freedom for Lewis?

Individual Activity: What I Want to Remember

Complete this activity on your own.

◊ Briefly review the readings and any notes you took.

◊ In the space below, write down the most significant thing you gained in this session—from your reading, video content, or discussion material.

What I want to remember from this session . . .

Closing Prayer

Close your time together in prayer.

Session 2 Personal Study

Reflect further by exploring additional material from *Mere Christianity* and Scripture.

Book 1, Chapter 5: We Have Cause to Be Uneasy

Lewis concludes Book 1 of *Mere Christianity* with chapter five, in which he notes that some readers may be turned off by the fact that it is now clear he is going to speak about religion. He comments that they may even feel as though he has tricked them by seeming at first like he was going to talk about philosophy when all along this has been just another "religious jaw" (28).

Lewis notes that part of his audience may have been prepared to listen to him as long as they thought he had something new to say, but if his topic is only going to be religion, their feeling is that the world has already tried that.

Here Lewis refers to the fact that many Britons, even in the 1940s, considered their culture to be post-Christian in the sense that it had tried Christianity, had found it somehow inadequate, and had now moved beyond it. For them, any discussion of Christianity—or even of religion in general—was a waste of time because the world, at least the modern world, was past all that. Lewis, however, reminds his readers that, so far, he has not said anything to promote the Bible or the church or religion but is trying, as he puts it, to see what we can learn from the world and our common humanity.

Question 1. G. K. Chesterton once wrote, "The Christian ideal has not been tried and found wanting. It has been found difficult; and left untried." Do you know of people who are willing to talk about philosophy, or any other topic, but put up barriers to Christianity because they think it has failed them? What would you say to someone who is not interested in anything having to do with Christianity because that would be, as Lewis puts it, trying to "put the clock back"?

With the end of chapter five, we conclude Book 1 in *Mere Christianity*, a book Lewis titles "Right and Wrong as a Clue to the Meaning of the Universe." Here Lewis is not claiming that our sense of right and wrong constitutes a formal proof for God, but rather that our sense of right and wrong is more like a signpost. It gives us a *clue* about the universe. In an essay titled "Simply Lewis: Reflections on a Master Apologist After 60 Years," N. T. Wright maintains that the value of this first book lies "not in the fact that it makes a convincing argument as such, but that it highlights features of human existence that are puzzling and interesting and point beyond themselves."

Question 2. Do you agree with this distinction between a *proof* for God and a *clue* about what is behind the universe? How strong a clue do you find our universal sense of right and wrong to be? Are there other clues that you might point to?

Question 3. In the title of chapter five, Lewis points out that "we have cause to be uneasy." Throughout Book 1, he has been making two points: that we, as humans, have insider knowledge that we ought to behave to a certain standard *and* that we all fail to live up to this standard. What does Scripture have to say about our fallen nature in verses such as Romans 1:18–21 and Romans 3:23? In what way does your own fallen nature most often rear its ugly head?

Reading Assignment

In preparation for Session 3, read:

- ◊ Book 2, Chapter 1: "The Rival Conceptions of God"
- ◊ Book 2, Chapter 2: "The Invasion"

3

The Rival Conceptions of God

Reading Assignment

In preparation for Session 3, read:

- ◊ Book 2, Chapter 1: "The Rival Conceptions of God"
- ◊ Book 2, Chapter 2: "The Invasion"

Watch Video: The *Rival Conceptions of God*

Play the video segment for Session 3. As you watch, take any notes that might be helpful to you in the space provided below.

Notes

Video Discussion

Book 2, Chapter 1: The Rival Conceptions of God

On January 11, 1942—a little more than five months after giving his first talk—C. S. Lewis was back by popular demand at BBC Headquarters in London. Once again the "On the Air" light flashed, and once again Lewis spoke to the nation.

When Lewis began this second set of talks, he could not assume that all of his listeners had heard the first series, so he began again by briefly introducing himself—an introduction which was removed when the talk appeared in book form. Lewis began by noting that it was not because he was anybody special that he was asked to speak about what Christians believe but that he was quite the opposite.

"They've asked me first of all because I'm a layman and not a parson, and consequently it was thought I might understand the ordinary person's point of view a bit better," Lewis told the audience. "Secondly, I think they asked me because it was known that I'd been an atheist for many years and only became a Christian quite fairly recently. They thought that would mean I'd be able to see the difficulties—able to remember what Christianity looks like from the outside."

Perhaps these two aspects, Lewis claimed, made him better able to explain what Christians believe.

> **Question 1.** What advantages would being a layman and a former atheist have given Lewis?

"I have been asked to tell you what Christians believe ..." With these ten words Lewis launched his second series of talks. These words also open Book 2 of *Mere Christianity.* But instead of starting with what Christians believe, Lewis chooses to begin with what they do *not* believe.

Atheists, Lewis notes, have to believe that the central point of all religions in the world is a huge mistake. By contrast, Christians do *not* have to believe that other religions are all wrong: even the strangest religion may contain a hint of the truth. That said, Lewis continues, being a Christian *does* mean "thinking that where Christianity differs from other religions, Christianity is right and they are wrong" (35). He observes that in this way faith is like arithmetic. There is only one right answer to an addition problem, but some of the wrong answers are much nearer being right than others.

> **Question 2.** At the start of Book 2 of *Mere Christianity*, Lewis explains that if you are a Christian you do not have to believe that all the other religions are simply wrong all through. Can you offer any examples of beliefs which Christianity has in common with other faiths? Why do you think Lewis began this way? What might make setting Christianity alongside other beliefs and finding similarities more effective than only stating what Christians believe?

Next Lewis takes us through the rival conceptions of God and points out several of the major divisions in beliefs. The first big division is between those people who believe in God and those who do not. Next Lewis moves on to show how the first group—those who believe in God—can be divided again according to what sort of God they believe in. Pantheists hold that God is in all material things and, in fact, does not exist apart from the material universe. According to pantheists, anything we find in the universe is a part of God, even cancer or a slum. Thus, to say that a slum or cancer is bad is to fail to see it from a proper, divine point of view.

Christians, Lewis explains, believe that God made the universe and exists apart from it. Yes, he put a great deal of himself into it, much like we can say that a painter may put a great deal of himself into a painting. But Christianity does not believe that God is the universe, any more than we would say that a painter is his painting.

> **Question 3.** Do you know people who believe that God is in everything, existing as part of the material universe? (This position is called pantheism.) How would you respond if they said that everything is divine? If Christians believe that God is also found in nature and in the material world around them, how would you explain the difference between that view and the pantheistic view?

Lewis concludes his chapter on "The Rival Conceptions of God" by presenting the Christian conception. Unlike the pantheists Lewis talked about, Christians believe that God has both created and is separate from the material world. He states that not everything in the universe is "good," no matter how proper our point of view. Some of the things in the world are actually *contrary* to God's will. Lewis notes that when he was an atheist, one argument he had against God was that the universe seemed unjust. But how had he got this idea of *just* and *unjust*? "A man does not call a line crooked unless he has some idea of a straight line," Lewis concludes (38).

As a young man, Lewis initially rejected any notion of God because he could not reconcile it with the unjust universe he saw around him. He was not merely complaining that the universe did not happen to please him, so God must not exist. More than that, the universe seemed unjust or unfair to all. Somewhere within him, Lewis had a deep and undeniable sense of justice by which he could measure things.

Lewis began *Mere Christianity* by pointing to people quarreling and the shared sense of right and wrong they need to have in order to have a quarrel. Here Lewis turns to a similar moral absolute: our inherent sense of justice. Yet, if the material universe is all there is, and it is a benign reality that simply is what it is, then where did this sense of justice come from?

> **Question 4.** Do you know people who do not believe in God but do believe in human rights and social justice—and not, as Lewis puts it, as private ideas of their own, but as absolute, universal principles? If you asked these people where or how they got their idea of justice, what might they say, and how might you answer them?

Book 2, Chapter 2: The Invasion

Lewis begins chapter two by noting that there is an over-simplistic version of Christianity which maintains that there is a good God in heaven and "everything is all right" (40). This, Lewis maintains, is *not* Christianity. Christianity is not simple, Lewis argues, nor can one expect it to be. Lewis notes that opponents to Christianity often put up "a version of Christianity suitable for a child of six" (41), and then make this the object of their attacks instead of the belief system that serious Christians hold. Lewis cautions readers to be on guard against these people who take as their target Christian beliefs which they have intentionally misrepresented.

Question 5. Have you met someone who tried to discredit Christianity by intentionally attacking a false, oversimplified version of it? What do you think is the best way to respond to this kind of attack on the faith?

In his book *Glimpsing the Face of God: The Search for Meaning in the Universe,* Alister McGrath writes: "Christian theology uses the language of 'fallenness' to describe this state of affairs. The world has fallen away from its God-given goals. All kinds of things have crept into the world to deflect it from its original purpose." Using words that parallel those of Lewis, McGrath concludes that our world is like a country that has been invaded by an occupying force, a country which "recalls its days of freedom in the past and eagerly awaits its liberation in the future."

From the start, Lewis has not tried to *prove* the Christian claims about God and the universe but rather to suggest that they make the most sense of the world we find ourselves in.

Question 6. In the video, Alister McGrath points out, "What Lewis is saying is that Christianity gives us a way of looking at the world around us and at looking at our own experience which makes sense of it." Why does it make sense to you, as a Christian, that we live in a good world that has gone wrong?

Individual Activity: What I Want to Remember

Complete this activity on your own.

◊ Briefly review the readings and any notes you took.

◊ In the space below, write down the most significant thing you gained in this session—from your reading, video content, or discussion material.

What I want to remember from this session . . .

Closing Prayer

Close your time together in prayer.

Session 3 Personal Study

Reflect further by exploring additional material from *Mere Christianity* and Scripture.

By his own admission, Lewis raises a problem in chapter two that is not a simple one: we exist in a universe that contains much that is indisputably bad and which also contains creatures who *know* that much of it is bad. The Christian explanation for these facts is that we live in a "good world that has gone wrong, but still retains the memory of what it ought to have been" (42).

Here Lewis addresses the objection raised in the previous chapter: "My argument against God was that the universe seemed so cruel and unjust" (38). The Christian answer is that the world is not the way it was meant to be. Instead, it is like a once beautiful city that is now ravaged by war—in this case a rebellion. And, Lewis maintains, we find ourselves in "a part of the universe that is occupied by the rebel" (45). We are, in essence, living in enemy-occupied territory.

"Badness is only spoiled goodness," Lewis writes. "And there must be something good first before it can be spoiled" (44).

> **Question 1.** In your own words, can you restate Lewis's point that evil is not an original condition but the perversion of a good condition created by God?

The invasion Lewis refers to in the chapter title comes from Christianity's claim that a good and perfect world has been invaded by a rebel force, and so now is corrupted or fallen. Lewis ends chapter two by observing that some readers are sure to ask if in today's modern age, he really is going reintroduce the devil here, a figure from ancient times with "horns and hoofs and all" (46).

Lewis responds with two points. First, he writes that he does not see what time—ancient or modern—has to do with it. And here Lewis revisits his earlier point on those who complain about putting back the clock. Lewis was a keen opponent of what he called Chronological Snobbery, the uncritical acceptance of current intellectual positions and the assumption that whatever has gone out of date has been refuted. In *Surprised by Joy*, Lewis describes the chronological snobbery he suffered from and tells readers that if a belief has gone out of date, rather than simply rejecting it, they must find out why it went out of date. Was it ever refuted? And if it was, then by whom and where and how conclusively? Perhaps the belief was never refuted but has merely gone out of fashion. "If the latter," Lewis concludes, "this tells us nothing about its truth or falsehood."

Secondly, Lewis suggests that his belief about the universe being an enemy-occupied territory has no connection to the horns and hoofs found in images of the devil. In *The Screwtape Letters*, Lewis addresses this same issue when the demon Screwtape offers his nephew the following advice for working with a patient: "If any faint suspicion of your existence begins to arise in his mind, suggest to him a picture of something in red tights, and persuade him that since he cannot believe in that (it is an old textbook method of confusing them) he therefore cannot believe in you."

Question 2. One of the objections to Christianity is that a two-thousand-year-old religion from the distant past can have little or nothing to say to people today. How would you respond to someone who rejected Christian beliefs—including its belief in a fallen angel and a fallen world—based on the claim that these beliefs are out of date?

Question 3. In "The Rival Conceptions of God," Lewis notes the difference between people who see Nature as an expression of God and those for whom Nature is God. How does Psalm 19:1—"The heavens declare the glory of God; the skies proclaim the work of his hands"—clarify this distinction? Can you think of other places in the Bible that talk about this topic?

Reading Assignment

In preparation for Session 4, read:

- ◊ Book 2, Chapter 3: "The Shocking Alternative"
- ◊ Book 2, Chapter 4: "The Perfect Penitent"

4

Free Will and the Shocking Alternative

Reading Assignment

In preparation for Session 4, read:

- ◊ Book 2, Chapter 3: "The Shocking Alternative"
- ◊ Book 2, Chapter 4: "The Perfect Penitent"

Watch Video: *Free Will and the Shocking Alternative*

Play the video segment for Session 4. As you watch, take any notes that might be helpful to you in the space provided.

Notes

Video Discussion

Book 2, Chapter 3: The Shocking Alternative

Lewis opens chapter three with a summary of the conclusion reached at the end of the previous chapter: "Christians, then, believe that an evil power has made himself for the present the Prince of this World" (47). He then raises the question of whether or not this situation is in accord with God's will. Certainly we would say that evil is contrary to God's will, but how can something happen that goes against the will of a being who is all-powerful? Here readers might be reminded of the point Lewis made a few pages earlier that it is no use asking for a simple religion.

Why does a good, all-powerful God allow evil to exist in such a prevalent way? Christianity's answer, Lewis explains, is that God wills for his creatures to be free to obey him or not. And given this freedom, some have chosen, and continue to choose, not to.

Is it possible to imagine a creature with free will but with no possibility of going wrong? Lewis writes about this question in *The Problem of Pain* where he asks whether it is possible for an all-powerful God "to give a creature free will and at the same time withhold free will from it." Omnipotence, Lewis concludes, does not mean being able to do something that is inherently impossible, in this case to both do it and not do it at the same time. Next Lewis points out that while he can conceive of a world where God countered each abuse of man's free will at the moment it happened—for example, by making a wooden beam about to be used as a weapon become as soft as grass—such a world would be one in which wrong actions would be impossible, so "freedom of the will would be void."

Here in *Mere Christianity*, Lewis reaches a similar conclusion, writing, "If a thing is free to be good it is also free to be bad" (48).

In the opening pages of chapter three, Lewis argues that the best explanation for the evil and wickedness in the world is that God wills for his creatures to have a choice of whether to obey him or not. In fact, we all—in ways large and small—have chosen not to obey and instead, as Lewis puts it, have chosen to put ourselves at the center and to be our own masters.

Question 1. In the video, Philip Yancey says, "Here is the Christian story in a nutshell. The world is good. The world is broken. The world can be and will be restored." How convincing do you find this summary of the reality we find around us? Are there other explanations you have heard? If so, how plausible do you think they are?

Having addressed the difficult problem of how evil can exist in a universe created by a good and all-powerful God, Lewis now turns to another difficult question. If free will is what makes evil possible, why did God give it to us? Why not just create a world full of humans who cannot disobey? Here Lewis suggests that God wanted beings that were distinct from himself instead of creatures that worked like machines or robots. A world of people who were simply puppets or robots would "hardly be worth creating" (48).

The question of why God gave humans free will when some were sure to abuse it is a difficult one. In *The Problem of Pain*, Lewis responds: "Once, before creation, it would have been true to say that everything was God. But God created: He caused things to be other than Himself that, being distinct, they might learn to love Him, and achieve union instead of mere sameness."

Lewis approaches the question from a slightly different angle in *God in the Dock* where he points out that God *could* forcibly alter people's characters if he wanted to. So why doesn't he? Lewis writes: "God has made it a rule for Himself that He won't alter people's character by force. He can and will alter them—but only if people let Him ... He would rather have a world of free beings, with all its risks, than a world of people who did right like machines because they couldn't do anything else."

Here in *Mere Christianity* Lewis sums up his point this way: "Free will, though it makes evil possible, is also the only thing that makes possible any love or goodness or joy worth having" (48). The happiness that God has designed us for is the happiness of being *voluntarily* united to him, and this means we must be free to choose.

Does this mean, then, that the existence of evil is in accordance with God's will? Only inasmuch as God wants his children to obey him because they love him and want to—not because they are forced to or have no other choice. In chapter three, Lewis draws a parallel between God and a mother with children who wants them to learn to do things on their own without her making them. The risk, then, is that children will do what is wrong. And, since we are living in "enemy-territory," the rebel may use our free will to corrupt and destroy.

Question 2. In the video, Philip Yancey puts it this way, "The reason God invented parents is so that we'd have an appreciation of what it's like to be God." Does this comparison work for you? How would you explain why God decided to give us free will?

So, God thought it was worth the price to have creatures with free will instead of a world of creatures who moved only when he pulled the strings. What, then, does going wrong look like? "The moment you have a self at all," Lewis writes, "there is a possibility of putting your self first" (49). Going wrong begins when we want to be our own master, when we want to put ourselves in God's place. But, Lewis maintains, history shows us that there is no way being our own masters will ever succeed. We will never find happiness or peace apart from God. We were meant to run on God, Lewis argues, like a car is made to run on gas.

Down through the centuries, Satan has tried to convince humans to try to find something other than God to make them happy. God, Lewis points out, has not been passive but, from the start, has been working to remedy the situation. First, he left us with a sense of right and wrong that, try as we might, we cannot get rid of. Second, he has haunted us with stories about a god who dies, then is risen, and through his own death gives humankind new life. Third, Lewis tells us, God chose one specific people, the Jews, to reveal himself to, particularly to reveal the facts that there is only one God and that he is concerned about right conduct.

Then finally among these Jews, a man appears who talks as if he were God, claiming that he has always existed, that he can forgive sins, and that at the end of time he will come again to judge the world. These are claims that, Lewis points out, were the "most shocking thing that has ever been uttered by human lips" (51). And here we come to one of the most famous quotes in *Mere Christianity*. Lewis writes:

> I am trying here to prevent anyone saying the really foolish thing that people often say about Him: "I'm ready to accept Jesus as a great moral teacher, but I don't accept His claim to be God." That is the one thing we must not say. A man who was merely a man and said the sort of things Jesus said would not be a great moral

> teacher. He would either be a lunatic—on a level with the man who says he is a poached egg—or else he would be the Devil of Hell. You must make your choice. Either this man was, and is, the Son of God: or else a madman or something worse. You can shut Him up for a fool, you can spit at Him and kill Him as a demon; or you can fall at His feet and call Him Lord and God. But let us not come with any patronizing nonsense about His being a great human teacher. He has not left that open to us. (52)

In this passage we find Lewis's famous Liar, Lunatic, or Lord trilemma. One of the most common objections to it is the claim that one other alternative is left open: the possibility that Christ was only a *legend*, not a historical figure who actually said the things which are recorded in the Gospels. But notice that Lewis begins with someone who is already past the legend option and is saying *I'm ready to accept Jesus as a great moral teacher.* This means that the person has already accepted the existence of a historical Jesus and has accepted the teachings ascribed to him as authentic—but wants to go no further.

Or we can fall at his feet and call him Lord and God. Lewis is not presenting a clever argument that we merely accept with our reason. He brings us to a radical conclusion with radical implications.

Question 3. In your own words, can you walk through Lewis's famous "Liar, Lunatic, or Lord" statement? After we have come to the decision that Jesus was *not* a legend, what are the only choices available to us?

> **Question 4.** In the video, Philip Yancey reports that although he later came to agree with Lewis, the first time he read this passage, he thought it was a gross exaggeration because he knew many people, including himself, who thought of Jesus as a great moral teacher and nothing else. How convincing or compelling do you find Lewis's conclusion to be?

If we believe that Lewis is correct and that Jesus is who he said he is, we must come to terms with the reality of his life, his death, and his resurrection. This is all really good news for a broken world. As Lewis puts it, mankind has got itself into a hole and in order to get out needs help from someone not in the hole. But what sort of hole is it? Lewis makes it clear that humans are not just imperfect creatures who simply need improvement here and there, but rebels who must lay down their arms. And this means nothing less than "surrendering, saying you are sorry, realizing that you have been on the wrong track and getting ready to start life over again from the ground floor" (56). Lewis argues that this surrender is not just eating humble pie but means unlearning all our self-conceit and self-will. It involves killing part of ourselves and experiencing a kind of death. The good news is that this submission and repentance is not demanded by God before he will take us back. It is what going back to him is like.

Lewis returns to this topic near the very end of *Mere Christianity* in the chapter titled "Nice People or New Men." There he points out that while redemption always improves someone, "mere improvement is not redemption" (216). Christ came to earth, suffered, and died not to produce better people of the old kind but to produce a new kind of person.

Question 5. Lewis compares repentance to a rebel laying down his arms—someone who had been trying to "set up on his own" and behaving "as if he belonged to himself" (56). He also compares repentance to starting life over again from the ground floor and to undergoing a kind of death. Do these comparisons match your own experience? Can you think of other images you might use to describe repentance?

Individual Activity: What I Want to Remember

Complete this activity on your own.

◊ Briefly review the readings and any notes you took.
◊ In the space below, write down the most significant thing you gained in this session—from your reading, video content, or discussion material.

What I want to remember from this session . . .

Closing Prayer

Close your time together in prayer.

Session 4 Personal Study

Reflect further by exploring additional material from *Mere Christianity* and Scripture.

Book 2, Chapter 4: The Perfect Penitent

At the start of chapter four, "The Perfect Penitent," Lewis restates his conclusion that Jesus was and is God, come to enemy-occupied earth in human form. Then he turns to the purpose of Christ's visit. "What did he come to do?" (53). Of course, Lewis points out, one reason that Jesus came was to teach, and certainly he spent a good deal of his time doing this. From Jesus we learn about the true nature of the kingdom of heaven, what God the Father is like, and how we are supposed to live. But as Lewis made clear, Jesus did not come to earth just to be a great teacher. Christianity claims that the main reason he came to earth was to suffer and be killed.

Why did Christ need to suffer and die? The Christian belief, Lewis points out, is that Christ's death "has somehow put us right with God" (54). The *somehow* in Lewis's statement is intentional as he points out there are a number of different theories of how Christ's death puts us right with God, and Christians do not all agree on which theory is the correct one. What all Christians do agree on is that Christ's death does put us right with God, that "it does work" (54).

In keeping with his emphasis on mere Christianity, the core beliefs shared by all Christians at all times, Lewis does not pick one particular theory to promote, and even goes so far as to say that it is Christ's atonement, not any particular atonement theory, that is important. "Theories about Christ's death are not Christianity," Lewis maintains. "They are explanations about how it works" (54). But knowing that Christians do not all agree even about how important accepting one particular theory is, Lewis notes that *from his viewpoint* the theories are not themselves the thing Christians are asked to accept, and he makes it clear that the observations in this section are how he personally looks at the matter. Lewis writes, "Any theories we build up as to how Christ's death did all this are, in my view, quite secondary" (56).

In fact, Lewis seems very content for the actual mechanism to remain a mystery. As John Piper observes in his essay "Lessons from an Inconsolable Soul," Lewis writes about the atonement "with reverence, but puts little significance on any of the explanations for how it actually saves sinners."

Question 1. Do you, or does your denomination, have a particular doctrine on how Christ's death works? Lewis suggests that just as someone can be nourished by his dinner without knowing exactly how, a person can accept what Christ has done without understanding how the atonement functions. How important or unimportant do you think it is that someone accepts a particular doctrine on this topic? To what extent, if any, do you think it is a mystery and can remain that way?

Lewis proposes a fundamental formula that Christians have to believe: Christ died for us; his death washes our sins away; and, by dying, Christ disabled death itself. And here it may be helpful to look at another place where Lewis presents this same formula but in a different way.

In *The Lion, the Witch and the Wardrobe,* Lewis shows Aslan giving his life for the traitor Edmund. There the White Witch tells Aslan, "You at least know the Magic which the Emperor put into Narnia at the very beginning. You know that every traitor belongs to me as my lawful prey and that for every treachery I have a right to kill."

After Aslan is killed on the Stone Table and returns to life, the great lion explains to Susan and Lucy that what the White Witch did not realize was that there was a deeper magic which said, "when a willing victim who had committed no treachery was killed in a traitor's stead, the Table would crack and Death itself would start working backward." We can say Aslan died for Edmund's sins or that Edmund was forgiven because Aslan did for him what he ought to have done. We can say that Aslan defeated death. We might even say that Edmund was washed in the blood of the lion. All these are true and are all different ways of expressing what took place.

In this passage from *The Chronicles of Narnia,* Aslan is—as the chapter title from *Mere Christianity* puts it—the perfect penitent, a willing victim who has committed no treachery. His death pays a ransom to the White Witch and removes her claim to the sinner Edmund and gives him a fresh start.

Question 2. Does Lewis's fictional depiction of atonement in Narnia help illustrate and bring to life Christ's atonement for us? If so, how?

When Jesus came to the region of Caesarea Philippi, he asked his disciples, "Who do people say the Son of Man is?"

They replied, "Some say John the Baptist; others say Elijah; and still others, Jeremiah or one of the prophets."

"But what about you?" he asked. "Who do you say I am?"

Simon Peter answered, "You are the Messiah, the Son of the living God."

Matthew 16:13–16

Question 3. *Who do you say I am?* This question is as important today as when Jesus first asked it. What does this passage from Matthew tell us about attitudes toward Jesus during his earthly ministry? To what extent are attitudes about Jesus today similar or different?

Reading Assignment

In preparation for Session 5, read:

◊ Book 3, Chapter 1: "The Three Parts of Morality"
◊ Book 3, Chapter 8: "The Great Sin"

5

Christian Behavior and the Great Sin of Pride

Reading Assignment

In preparation for Session 5, read:

- ◊ Book 3, Chapter 1: "The Three Parts of Morality"
- ◊ Book 3, Chapter 8: "The Great Sin"

Watch Video:
Christian Behavior and the Great Sin of Pride

Play the video segment for Session 5. As you watch, take any notes that might be helpful to you in the space provided.

Notes

Video Discussion

Book 3, Chapter 1: The Three Parts of Morality

In Book 2 of *Mere Christianity*, Lewis focused on Christian beliefs. In Book 3, he examines the implications of these beliefs as he turns to the topic of Christian behavior. Lewis notes that when we think of Christian behavior, we might mistakenly imagine that God is merely looking for strict obedience to a rigid set of rules. What God really wants, Lewis points out, are "people of a particular sort" (80), people who have developed the internal qualities traditionally known as virtues. Accordingly, Lewis devotes most of this book on Christian behavior to the seven virtues. He begins with the four Cardinal virtues—prudence, temperance, justice, and fortitude. Then he turns to the three Theological virtues—faith, hope, and charity. Sandwiched in between these virtues, Lewis takes time to talk about one particular vice.

Here in chapter one, "The Three Parts of Morality," Lewis begins with the story about a schoolboy who, when asked what he thought God was like, responded that as far as he could tell, God was "the sort of person who is always snooping around to see if anyone is enjoying himself and then trying to stop it" (69). Interestingly, later Lewis would go on to create a villain who fits this description perfectly: the White Witch in *The Lion, the Witch and the Wardrobe.*

For many people, Lewis notes, morality has this same mistaken image as something that interferes and stops people from having a good time. "In reality," Lewis writes, "moral rules are directions for running the human machine" (69). Each moral rule is designed to prevent a breakdown, a strain, or a friction that would occur without it.

Question 1. In the video, Diana Glyer points out that for Lewis, morality was more than just a checklist of negative behaviors. What can be done to help people see that moral rules are intended to help us, not hinder us?

Next Lewis presents the argument that morality is concerned with three things: our relationship to others, our internal condition, and our relationship to God. He notes that modern people nearly always focus on the first aspect and forget the other two. To help his readers better understand these three parts of morality, Lewis compares humans to a fleet of ships setting out on a voyage.

One way that both humans and ships can go wrong is when they collide or get in another's way. For the voyage to be a success, there must be rules to govern how ships work together to avoid collisions and do all kinds of damage to each other. A second type of problem that will prevent a successful voyage occurs if things go wrong inside one of the ships. As Lewis notes, each ship must be seaworthy and have its engines in good order if it is going to reach its destination.

The final aspect to take into account is where the fleet is trying to get to. However well the ships may sail—individually and collectively—the voyage will still be a failure if they arrive at the wrong place.

Lewis concludes chapter one by stating that when we think about Christian morality and Christian behavior, we need to think of all three parts: "relations between man and man, things inside each man, and relations between man and the power that made him" (75). Or as Diana Glyer puts it in the video, Lewis reminds us that "moral choices have to do with, not just getting along with others, or how I tidy up my own life, but how my life relates to the ultimate purpose of life." Near the end of chapter one, Lewis concludes that different beliefs about the universe will lead to different behavior.

Question 2. Besides being kind, honest, and helpful to others, what else does Christian morality require from us in terms of how we behave?

Book 3, Chapter 8: The Great Sin

Back in the chapter titled "The Perfect Penitent," Lewis pointed out that repentance means having to unlearn "all the self-conceit and self-will that we have been training ourselves into for thousands of years" (57). Here in chapter eight, Lewis further explores this self-conceit and self-will as he provides an in-depth look at the great sin of pride. While we may loathe pride when we see it in other people, Lewis points out that it is the one vice we all share. Pride, Lewis proposes, is the sin at the center of all other sin, the vice which "leads to every other vice" (122).

In claiming that pride is the essential vice and the utmost evil, Lewis writes that he is following the path of previous Christian teachers. One of the teachers Lewis has in mind here is Saint Augustine. In chapter five of *The Problem of Pain*, Lewis paraphrases Augustine's definition of pride, referring to it as "the movement whereby a creature ... tries to set up on its own, to exist for itself." Lewis then summarizes mankind's fallen condition this way: "We try, when we wake, to lay the new day at God's feet; before we have finished shaving, it becomes *our* day and God's share in it is felt as a tribute which we must pay out of 'our own' pocket."

Here in *Mere Christianity* Lewis argues that pride—setting up ourselves at the center in God's rightful place—is the sin through which the Devil became the devil and the "complete anti-God state of mind" (122).

Question 3. As Diana Glyer explains in the video, Lewis saw pride like the foundation of a building, at the base of all other sins. Lewis then asks us if this claim seems exaggerated. What do you think? As Lewis describes it here, does his claim that pride is the great sin make sense to you? Why or why not?

Lewis next turns to spiritual pride, the pleasure of thinking you are more godly than, or morally superior to, others. "It is a terrible thing," Lewis notes, "that the worst of all the vices can smuggle itself into the very center of our religious life" (125). How is it, Lewis asks, that people who are eaten up by pride can claim to believe in God and are able to appear to themselves as very religious? Lewis proposes that while, in theory, these people admit to God that they are nothing, all the time they are really imagining "how God approves of them and thinks them far better than ordinary people" (124).

In letter twenty-four of *The Screwtape Letters*, Screwtape refers to spiritual pride as "the strongest and most beautiful" of all the vices, meaning that from the divine perspective it is the ugliest. The senior devil instructs his pupil, Wormwood, to nurture the feeling of *how different we Christians are* in his patient, and by *we Christians* he must really mean *my set of Christians*, which becomes by extension the feeling of *how different I am*.

Lewis writes in chapter eight that if we ever discover that our religious life is making us feel we are better than others, we can be sure that these feelings are not from God but from the devil. The real test of being close to God, Lewis proposes, is that we either forget about ourselves altogether or see ourselves as small and dirty—and the former position, forgetting about ourselves altogether, is better.

In the parable of the Pharisee and the tax collector, Christ provides a compelling portrait of spiritual pride (Luke 18:10–13). The Pharisee stands up in front of everyone and prays, "God, I thank you that I am not like other people—robbers, evildoers, adulterers—or even like this tax collector. I fast twice a week and give a tenth of all I get." The tax collector will not even raise his eyes to heaven but beats on his breast and simply prays, "God, have mercy on me, a sinner."

Question 4. How does spiritual pride show itself in you—or in others? Why are we often blind to our own spiritual pride? Why do you think it can be so hard to see? In what ways might we combat it?

Before leaving the topic of pride, Lewis wants to clear up four possible misunderstandings. The first is that "pleasure in being praised is not pride" (125). From the child who has done a particularly good job on his homework to the soul to whom Christ says, "Well done"—Lewis argues that we ought to take pleasure in having pleased someone we rightly wanted to please. The sin of pride enters in only when we start thinking, "What a fine person I must be to have done it" (126).

The second misconception has to do with whether being proud of a child, a parent, one's school, or one's military regiment is a sin. Lewis's answer is that it depends on what we mean by *being proud of.* If *being proud of* means *having a warmhearted admiration for,* then this, Lewis notes, is "very far away from being a sin" (127). But being puffed up because we belong to a distinguished group or have a famous family member is a fault; although, Lewis notes, it is still better than being puffed up about our own accomplishments or attributes.

A third misconception would be to think of God as a petty potentate who demands that we humble ourselves before him so his dignity will not be offended. As Lewis observes, God is "not in the least worried about his dignity" (127). Lewis points to the delightful relief that comes when we get rid of all the silly nonsense about our own dignity which has made us restless and unhappy all our lives. What a comfort it is, Lewis writes, to stop all the posturing and posing, to drop the endless cries of "Look at me."

The fourth and final misconception has to do with what it means to be humble. Lewis tells us not to imagine a "greasy, smarmy person" who goes around telling everyone how he is nobody (128). Instead, truly humble people might impress us with the way that they really listen to others and seem to enjoy life so easily. The humble person, Lewis notes, will not be thinking all the time about how humble he is—in fact, he will not be thinking much about himself at all. Lewis expands on this point in letter fourteen of *The Screwtape Letters*, where Screwtape tells Wormwood he must hide the true nature of humility from his patient. "Let him think of it not as self-forgetfulness but a certain kind of opinion (namely, a low opinion) of his own talents and character." Through this deception, Screwtape observes, "Thousands of humans have been brought to think that humility means pretty women trying to believe they are ugly and clever men trying to believe they are fools."

Screwtape concludes by noting that God, referred to as the Enemy, has a very different goal for mankind. He tells Wormwood that God wants to restore to his children a "new kind of self-love" that causes them to rejoice in the talents they have been given "as frankly and gratefully" as they do in their neighbor's talents.

Question 5. Diana Glyer states in the video, "To feel good about oneself or to have self-esteem isn't the same as pride." Are there other ways that we misconstrue what it means to be proud or what it means to be humble? What is your response to one or more of the misconceptions about pride and humility that Lewis presents? Lewis argues that the opposite of pride is humble self-forgetfulness. Do you think people today are any more or less focused on themselves than they were in the past?

Individual Activity: What I Want to Remember

Complete this activity on your own.

◊ Briefly review the readings and any notes you took.
◊ In the space below, write down the most significant thing you gained in this session—from your reading, video content, or discussion material.

What I want to remember from this session . . .

Closing Prayer

Close your time together in prayer.

Session 5 Personal Study

Reflect further by exploring additional material from *Mere Christianity* and Scripture.

Lewis points out that pride can be nearly impossible to see in ourselves. Having been blind to his own pride for many years, Lewis became more and more aware of his pride as he came closer to converting to Christianity. On January 30, 1930—in between his conversion to theism and his acceptance of Christ—Lewis wrote to a friend describing what he now saw when he examined himself and confessed that he was disturbed by the pride he had discovered. Lewis reported:

> During my afternoon "meditations"—which I at least *attempt* quite regularly now—I have found out ludicrous and terrible things about my own character. Sitting by, watching the rising thoughts ... one out of every three is a thought of self-admiration ... I catch myself posturing before the mirror, so to speak, all day long. I pretend I am carefully thinking out what to say to the next pupil (for *his* good, of course) and then suddenly realize I am really thinking how frightfully clever I'm going to be and how he will admire me. I pretend I am remembering an evening of good fellowship in a really friendly and charitable spirit—and all the time I'm really remembering how good a fellow I am and how well I talked. And then when you force yourself to stop it, you admire yourself for doing *that* ... There seems to be no end to it. Depth under depth of self-love and self-admiration.

Depth under depth of self-love and self-admiration. In *The Voyage of the Dawn Treader*, Lewis shows us a fictional character, Eustace, who must confront layer after layer of pride until he at last is able to see how "dragonish" he has been for most of his life. Finally desiring to change, Eustace—who has literally turned into a dragon by then—is able to shed the superficial layers, or skins, of his dragon nature somewhat easily, without much pain, and without any help. The deeper layers are just the opposite. Eustace finds they are impossible to remove on his own. He cannot un-dragon himself. He needs Aslan to do it for him.

"The very first tear he made was so deep that I thought it had gone right into my heart," Eustace reports to Edmund afterward. "And when he began pulling the skin off, it hurt worse than anything I've ever felt. The only thing that made me able to bear it was just the pleasure of feeling the stuff peel off."

In *Born Again*, the best-selling story of his conversion, Chuck Colson, former special counsel to President Nixon and founder of Prison Fellowship Ministries, recounts the effect that this chapter on pride from *Mere Christianity* had on him. As a friend named Tom read the chapter aloud, Colson reports that key events in his life paraded before him as if they were projected on a screen: his graduation speech, marrying into a prestigious family, being named as one of the outstanding young men of Boston, and finally being appointed to a powerful position in the White House.

"Now, sitting there on the dimly lit porch, my self-centered past was washing over me in waves," Colson writes. "It was painful. Agony. Desperately I tried to defend myself ... It was pride—Lewis's 'great sin'—that had propelled me through life."

> **Question 1.** In Chuck Colson, Eustace, and Lewis himself, we see how devious pride can be and how deep it can run. As Lewis observed, there seems to be no end of it. What about you? Have you had moments when you were able to see yourself as you really are and discovered the great sin of pride? What was it that finally allowed you to see it?

Next Lewis turns to the nature of pride and explains how pride is essentially competitive. "It is because I wanted to be the big noise at the party that I am so annoyed at someone else being the big noise," Lewis explains (122). The proud person, Lewis observes, gets no pleasure from merely having something, but rather out of having more of it than the next person—and this distinction is critical.

In a chapter from *The Taste for the Other* (aptly titled "The Sweet Poison of the False Infinite"), Gilbert Meilaender argues that the question of our proper stance toward the things of creation is one Lewis returns to often. Lewis's answer, Meilaender asserts, is that we are to have deep enjoyment but not slavish adoration of things—and both parts of the formula are important. Just as it is wrong to take pleasure out of having more than the next person, at the same time it is wrong not to find pleasure and take delight in the good things God has given us.

In *Miracles*, Lewis maintains that we are to give the things of this world "neither worship nor contempt." In his essay "A Slip of the Tongue," he argues that in the life of a perfect believer, feasts would be considered just as Christian as fasts. In chapter seven of *The Lion, the Witch and the Wardrobe*, the four Pevensie children join Mr. and Mrs. Beaver for a delicious meal. The narrator reports there are boiled potatoes with "a great big lump of deep yellow butter" from which everyone can take "as much as he wanted." The main course is "good freshwater fish" followed by "a great and gloriously sticky marmalade roll" fresh from the oven and steaming hot. Afterward, they each have a big cup of tea, push back their stools, and let out "a long sigh of contentment." Lewis makes it clear that their enjoyment is a proper enjoyment because they take pleasure in the dinner itself, not because it was better than the meal the Beavers' next-door neighbors were eating that night.

In chapter five of *The Voyage of the Dawn Treader*, Lewis provides another example of proper enjoyment. The character Lucy believes she is the most fortunate girl in the world as she wakes each morning to see "reflections of the sunlit water dancing on the ceiling of her cabin" and "all the nice new things she had got in the Lone Islands—seaboots and buskins and cloaks and jerkins and scarves." Here Lucy delights in her new garments because they are nice, not because they are nicer than the ones other girls have.

The deep and proper satisfaction found in these two scenes contrasts with the lack of contentment found in the proud person Lewis describes in *Mere Christianity*, the person who "even when he has got more than he can possibly want, will try to get still more" (123).

Question 2. Can you point to something you take a proper pleasure in? Can you point to an area where, because of pride, you always compare yourself with others?

To some who were confident of their own righteousness and looked down on everyone else, Jesus told this parable: "Two men went up to the temple to pray, one a Pharisee and the other a tax collector. The Pharisee stood by himself and prayed: 'God, I thank you that I am not like other people—robbers, evildoers, adulterers—or even like this tax collector. I fast twice a week and give a tenth of all I get.'

"But the tax collector stood at a distance. He would not even look up to heaven, but beat his breast and said, 'God, have mercy on me, a sinner.'

"I tell you that this man, rather than the other, went home justified before God. For all those who exalt themselves will be humbled, and those who humble themselves will be exalted."

Luke 18:9–14

Question 3. Lewis writes that as long as you are proud, you cannot know God. What does the parable of the Pharisee and the tax collector reveal about the nature of pride and about real humility?

Reading Assignment

In preparation for Session 6, read:

◊ Book 3, Chapter 10: "Hope"

6

The Christian Virtue of Hope

Reading Assignment

In preparation for Session 6, read:

- ◊ Book 3, Chapter 10: "Hope"

Watch Video: *The Christian Virtue of Hope*

Play the video segment for Session 6. As you watch, take any notes that might be helpful to you in the space provided.

Notes

Video Discussion

Book 3, Chapter 10: Hope

In this chapter about the Christian virtue of hope, Lewis begins by noting what hope is not. Christian hope is not escapism or wishful thinking. Our "continual looking forward to the eternal world" does not mean that we are to leave the present world as it is (134). Lewis writes that despite the fact that heaven, not earth, is our true, eternal home, Christians have an obligation to try to make our temporary home a better place.

Lewis takes up this same topic in the essay "Some Thoughts," where he argues that except for a church, there is no building more self-explanatory than a Christian hospital. From its inception, Christianity has been assigned the tasks of healing the sick and caring for the poor. Lewis goes on to explain that since Christians see this world as God's creation, they will fight against all blemishes upon it, including "pain and poverty, barbarism and ignorance."

In the *Mere Christianity* chapter on charity, Lewis notes that we are to love and care for our neighbors whether we have affectionate feelings for them or not. Here in chapter ten he points to a number of improvements in society that Christians have brought about. A primary example is the abolition of the slave trade in England. A group of English Evangelicals, among them William Wilberforce and John Newton, rejected the notion that slaves were supposed to accept their lot in life as property and set their sights on heaven. The Evangelicals argued that slaves were not property but fellow human beings created in the image of God, and they worked tirelessly to change the laws of England to abolish the slave trade. They succeeded.

In the video, Philip Yancey mentions the old Southern Gospel song that goes, "This world is not my home. I'm just a passin' through." He points out the problem of focusing only on "pie in the sky" and states that Lewis was a master at bringing the two worlds—this one and the next—together.

Question 1. Why do you think Lewis felt the need to point out our duty to improve this world and not merely set our sights on the next? Have you ever known someone who needed this correction, or have you yourself ever needed it? At the same time, is it possible for Christians to become too focused on changing this world?

Next Lewis turns to the relationship between the earthly pleasures that promise fulfillment—a new love, beautiful scenery, an exciting new interest—and the otherworldly longing we experience. Lewis proposes, and he makes it clear this is only speculation, that these earthly pleasures were never meant to satisfy this desire but only to arouse it and to suggest the real thing. If this is true, then our attitude toward these earthly blessings must be dual-natured. We must not despise or be ungrateful for them, but we also must not mistake them for this "something else" of which they are "only a kind of copy, or echo, or mirage" (137).

In chapter ten of *The Problem of Pain*, Lewis lists various ways this deep longing may come to us—including cherished books, certain landscapes, and favorite hobbies—and notes that these are all only vehicles, not the true object of our desire. Lewis continues:

> Tantalizing glimpses, promises never quite fulfilled, echoes that died away just as they caught your ear. But if it should really become manifest—if there ever came an echo that did not die away but swelled into the sound itself—you would know it. Beyond all possibility of doubt you would say, "Here at last is the thing I was made for."

In "The Weight of Glory," Lewis makes the same point: the cravings of our hearts may be stirred up by this world but will never be satisfied by this world. Lewis comments, "These things ... are good images of what we really desire; but if they are mistaken for the thing itself, they turn into dumb idols, breaking the hearts of their worshipers. For they are not the thing itself; they are only the scent of a flower we have not found, the echo of the tune we have not heard, news from a country we have never yet visited."

> **Question 2.** In the video, Philip Yancey says that when he experienced the beauty of nature—wildflowers in the wilderness and gorgeous tropical reefs in the ocean—he felt gratitude and wanted to know the artist. Has a beautiful sunset, a certain landscape, a favorite book, or a piece of music ever aroused a longing in you that went beyond scenery, books, or music? Are there other ways that this deep longing has come to you?

So what do we do about this strange craving? Here in chapter ten Lewis describes three ways of responding to the situation we find ourselves in. The first, which he calls the Fool's Way, is to blame the things themselves. Since this love, or job, or vacation was not able to satisfy the deep longing we feel for something more, the answer is simply to find someone else to love, a different place to travel, a new job, and so on. And of course when these new things once more fail to satisfy us, we try again, each time looking to find a better spouse, a more expensive destination, a more interesting job—and we might add a more luxurious house, a flashier car, a more expensive watch, or a bigger diamond—each time thinking that this time we will find what we have been searching for.

The second response Lewis describes is the way of the Disillusioned, so-called Sensible Man, who says that this fulfillment we have been longing for is just "moonshine" (136). It simply does not exist, for there is nothing that is going to truly satisfy us. While naïve and starry-eyed young people may hold on to the belief that there must be something out there that can fulfill this desire, those who are older and more experienced will have learned better and will have lowered their expectations.

Lewis concludes with a third way to confront this longing that nothing in this world can satisfy—the Christian's Way. In one of the most famous sentences from *Mere Christianity* Lewis writes: "If I find in myself a desire which no experience in this world can satisfy, the most probable explanation is that I was made for another world" (136–37). It is worth noting that Lewis is not claiming here that this desire *proves* we are made for another world. This longing, like our sense of right and wrong, is a clue that leads to a probable explanation.

Rather than trying to ignore or quench this desire as the "Sensible Man" does, Christians are to do the exact opposite. Although other interests may try to turn it aside or snow it under, we are to work to keep alive in ourselves this desire for our true country. We are to make pressing on to this other country, and helping others to press on, the main object of our lives.

Question 3. Philip Yancey points out in the video that the more we turn to earthly pleasures to satisfy our deep spiritual longing, the more we crave—until eventually we become their slaves. Saint Augustine has written, "Our hearts are restless until they rest in [God]." Besides travel, romance, and work, where else do people look, hoping to fill the God-shaped hole in their hearts?

Question 4. Briefly outline the three ways Lewis says we can respond to our lack of satisfaction. Have you known people who followed the Fool's Way or the Way of the Disillusioned "Sensible Man"? Have you followed either of these two ways at any point in your own life?

If one reason some Christians find it hard to want heaven is because we have been trained to fix our minds on this world, Lewis closes chapter ten with a second reason: the thought that we will spend eternity playing harps and walking streets of gold. Lewis comments on the silliness of trying to take literally the symbolic language used in Scripture to describe heaven—the harps, crowns, and golden streets. These are metaphors, he says—an attempt "to express the inexpressible," that which defies description (137).

Question 5. In Revelation 21:21 we are told that the main street in heaven is made of pure gold. What other symbolic images have been associated with heaven? How can we describe our hope of heaven in ways that are engaging and meaningful to non-Christians?

Individual Activity: What I Want to Remember

Complete this activity on your own.

- ◊ Briefly review the readings and any notes you took.
- ◊ In the space below, write down the most significant thing you gained in this session—from your reading, video content, or discussion material.

What I want to remember from this session . . .

Closing Prayer

Close your time together in prayer.

Session 6 Personal Study

Reflect further by exploring additional material from *Mere Christianity* and Scripture.

One of the central themes that run throughout nearly all Lewis's writing is the deep, insatiable longing that seems to be built in each of us. There are all kinds of things in this world, Lewis observes, that promise to fulfill this ingrained longing—things such as falling in love, traveling to a new country, starting a new job, or learning a new subject. The problem, Lewis maintains, is that "they never quite keep their promise" (135). No matter how good the husband or wife, how excellent the hotels and scenery, or how interesting the new job or new subject, the initial excitement always fades, leaving us still feeling a deep desire for something that we cannot quite put our finger on.

In his autobiography, *Surprised by Joy*, one of the first things that Lewis makes clear is that by *Joy*—always spelled with a capital "J"—he does not mean *joy* in the normal sense of happiness or elation. Lewis uses *Joy* to refer to the strange, intense longing he felt, beginning in childhood and continuing throughout his life. Lewis writes, "It was a sensation, of course, of desire; but a desire for what?... Before I knew what I desired, the desire itself was gone, the whole glimpse withdrawn, the world turned commonplace again." Although he did not know what this desire was for or where it came from, Lewis knew one thing: it was very powerful, so powerful that he finds it hard to come up with words strong enough to describe it. One thing he can tell us is that anyone who has experienced it will want it again. There is bliss in this deep longing. At the same time it is also colored by a feeling of sadness or sorrow, but this sadness is a kind that we want, for this unsatisfied desire is "more desirable than any other satisfaction."

In "The Weight of Glory," Lewis refers to this mysterious longing as a desire for a "far-off country," a yearning for "something that has never actually appeared in our experience." Lewis writes about this feeling in *The Problem of Pain* as well, where he refers to it as "that something which you were born desiring" and the thing that we were made for.

Lewis began *Mere Christianity* with the observation that people quarreling proves we are born with a sense of right and wrong. Here in chapter ten he offers another general observation, claiming that if people truly looked into their hearts, they would realize that they want "something that cannot be had in this world" (135).

Question 1. Can you identify with the experience of mysterious longing that Lewis writes about both in chapter ten of *Mere Christianity* and elsewhere—this longing that nothing in this world can satisfy? Have you felt it yourself? How would you describe it?

Lewis came to identify this inconsolable longing—which haunted and disturbed him, in the best sense, all through his life—as a longing for heaven, our true home. And as has been mentioned, he wrote about this topic in a number of places, nowhere more powerfully than in *The Chronicles of Narnia.*

In *The Voyage of the Dawn Treader,* a book that Lewis once said was about the spiritual life, Reepicheep tells Lucy and Edmund about the strange verse that was said over him while he was in his cradle and cast a mysterious spell upon him:

> Where sky and water meet,
> Where the waves grow sweet,
> Doubt not, Reepicheep,
> To find all you seek,
> There is the utter East.

As the valiant mouse discovers in the final chapter, what he has been longing for all his life is to journey to Aslan's Country. As he sails in his tiny coracle over the giant standing wave that lies at the end of the world where sky and water meet, he has no doubts that he is about to find what he has been seeking.

At the end of *The Last Battle,* Jewel the Unicorn gives voice to related thoughts. Upon reaching the new Narnia, Jewel declares: "I have come home at last! This is my real country! I belong here. This is the land I have been looking for all my life, though I never knew it till now."

Have you, like Reepicheep, ever felt as though a spell of longing for another world has been put upon you? In "The Weight of Glory," Lewis points out that spells are used for "breaking enchantments as well as for inducing them" and then suggests that humans have need of "the strongest spell that can be found" to wake us from the enchantment of worldliness which tries to convince us that our ultimate good is to be found in the things of this world and to silence the quiet, inner voice that says otherwise.

Question 2. Here in chapter ten of *Mere Christianity*, Lewis writes that the whole focus of our education tends "to fix our minds on this world" (135). What has helped to break the enchantment of worldliness in your life?

Question 3. The apostle Paul writes: "But our citizenship is in heaven. And we eagerly await a Savior from there, the Lord Jesus Christ" (Philippians 3:20). What does heavenly citizenship mean to you? How do you personally live with the present and future tensions that Paul describes here?

Reading Assignment

In preparation for Session 7, read:

◊ Book 4, Chapter 1: "Making and Begetting"
◊ Book 4, Chapter 2: "The Three-Personal God"

7

God in Three Persons

Reading Assignment

In preparation for Session 7, read:

- ◊ Book 4, Chapter 1: "Making and Begetting"
- ◊ Book 4, Chapter 2: "The Three-Personal God"

Watch Video: *God in Three Persons*

Play the video segment for Session 7. As you watch, take any notes that might be helpful to you in the space provided.

Notes

Video Discussion

Book 4, Chapter 1: Making and Begetting

Everyone has warned me not to tell you what I am going to tell you in this last book.

So begins "Beyond Personality," the fourth and final section of *Mere Christianity.*

In Book 1, Lewis focused on something everyone has experienced—our shared sense of right and wrong and the clue it provides to the meaning of the universe. In Book 2, Lewis showed how Christian beliefs provide a satisfying explanation for our experience. In Book 3, he examined Christian behavior. Now in Book 4, Lewis turns to theological doctrines of Christianity and in chapter one presents the first step in the doctrine of the Trinity: the distinction between making and begetting.

Here Lewis disregards the advice he was given to stick with plain, practical religion because, in his opinion, anyone wanting to think about God would want to have the clearest and the most accurate ideas available. So, despite having been advised that his readers are not interested in theology, Lewis says he has no desire to treat them like children. He reminds them (and us) that Christianity "claims to be telling us about another world"—life on the divine level—so some of its claims are bound to be difficult (156).

Question 1. Lewis waits until the final book of *Mere Christianity* to bring up the more complicated doctrines of the faith. Why do you think he waited until the end of the book to do so? Do you think that today people in general are less interested in theology, and in books like *Mere Christianity*, than they were in the past? If so, why? Is there a proper time and place to discuss such weighty topics? If so, when and where?

In the kind of honesty that makes *Mere Christianity* so effective, Lewis admits, "In a way I quite understand why some people are put off by Theology" (153). He then recounts the story of an officer in the R.A.F. who told of feeling God's presence in the desert at night. The officer said that, compared to this experience, the Christian creeds seemed petty, pedantic, and unreal.

Lewis agrees that theology is always going to be less real than the God it tells us about, just as a map of the Atlantic Ocean is going to be less real than standing on the beach and looking out to sea. "Doctrines are not God," Lewis writes, "they are only a kind of map" (154). But if we want to get any further on our journey, Lewis argues, we are going to need a map, and the doctrines of Christianity are a map based on the experience of many people who really knew God.

> **Question 2.** In the video, Joseph Pearce underscores Lewis's point that theology is not only practical, it is necessary—for unless we are anchored in orthodox doctrine, it is possible to drift off in all sorts of strange directions. Lewis writes that we need both the experience of God and the map of theology. Do you know someone who is missing one of these aspects? Has there been a time in your own life when one of these aspects—doctrine or personal experience—has been more needed than the other?

Next Lewis reminds those readers who still may not be convinced of their need for theology that anyone who wants to ignore talking about Christian doctrines will still have ideas about God, and many of these ideas will be wrong or muddled and may even be ideas that were "tried centuries ago and rejected" (155).

Lewis maintains that theology is both practical and necessary—especially now when everyone is exposed to all sorts of ideas about God. He points out that someone who rejects any contact with Christian concepts about God will have contact only with non-Christian ones—and this limitation will be problematic.

Question 3. Have you ever known someone who is interested in ideas about God as long as they are not Christian ideas? What might have caused this bias? How might you reach someone like this?

Book 4, Chapter 2: The Three-Personal God

Lewis writes that it is only Christians who have any idea of "how human souls can be taken into the life of God and yet remain themselves" (161). In fact, Lewis points out, as we are taken up into the life of God, we become even more ourselves than we were before. And he sees this idea of being taken into the life of God but still remaining separate as a key to understanding the Trinity.

A three-person God—how can this be? Lewis uses the idea of a cube to help us imagine how the Father, Son, and Holy Spirit can be one God and yet three separate persons. On a flat sheet of paper, two squares will always be two separate figures. But if we go from two dimensions to three, we can see how six separate squares can be joined into one cube. The squares never cease to exist. They are not absorbed into the cube like a drop of water into the ocean. They remain six separate squares combined into one cube.

On the divine level, Lewis proposes, we still find distinct personalities, but we find them combined in new ways which are hard or impossible for us to comprehend. Here in chapter two he uses the analogy of a cube with six sides. In chapter four, Lewis will use the image of two books that have been lying on a table for ever and ever, one on top of the other to show how the Son has always been co-eternal with the Father and at the same time has always been dependent, or resting, upon him.

> **Question 4.** Do Lewis's images help you make sense of the doctrine of the Trinity? Why or why not? Are there other analogies you have found helpful in understanding how God can be three persons in one? How important is it for us to understand the doctrine of the Trinity; to what extent can it remain a mystery?

Lewis began Book 4 with the story of the R.A.F. officer's encounter with God. He closes chapter two by returning to experience, not the experience of a single individual but that of the entire Christian community expressed in the form of Christian tradition. The doctrine of the Trinity, Lewis points out, is "not something we have made up" but has come from our collective perception of God as he reveals himself to us (164).

What is the good of talking about a three-person God we cannot fully conceive of? Well, talking about him is not the point, Lewis tells us. The whole point or goal of theology is to help bring us to the thing that matters, which is "being actually drawn into that three-personal life" (163). And here we come full circle. It is because our experience of God is so central that having a map to guide us is so important. And we need not have a thorough knowledge of Christian theology before we can start our journey and begin to be drawn into communion with God. "That may begin anytime," Lewis reminds us. "Tonight, if you like" (163).

So what are people to do if they want to be drawn into closer communion with God? Lewis points to an ordinary Christian kneeling in prayer. It is here, he claims, that we are "pulled into God, by God" while still remaining ourselves (163).

In his book *Miracles*, Lewis notes that our reason and imagination have important roles to play in our effort to know God, but it is in our devotional life that "we touch something concrete" which goes beyond abstraction. Lewis points to the invitation from Psalm 34:8, "Taste and see!" Theology is intended to lead us to a deeper, more real life in God, not substitute for it.

Question 5. How have you found studying the Christian doctrines to be helpful to your faith? Has studying theology ever detracted from your faith? If so, how?

In October, 1958—six years after the release of *Mere Christianity*—an article appeared in *The Christian Century* titled "Apologist Versus Apologist: A Critique of C. S. Lewis as 'Defender of the Faith.'" In it Norman Pittenger, a professor at General Theological Seminary, criticized Lewis for a number of reasons. Among Lewis's supposed faults was his "inept illustration" of the Trinity as a cube made of separate squares, which Pittenger saw as "vulgar"—in the sense that it lacked appropriate refinement.

Lewis penned a "Rejoinder to Dr. Pittenger" in which he admitted to the truth of some of Pittenger's criticisms but defended himself on others. About his decision to use the analogy of a cube, Lewis said that he could not see why an illustration from geometry should be considered offensive. And even if the image was lacking in taste or refinement, Lewis argued, what did it matter "if it gets across to the unbeliever what the unbeliever desperately needs to know?"

Lewis concluded with an explanation of what he was trying to do in his Christian apologetics, the audience he was writing for, and the problem he was trying to address.

> When I began, Christianity came before the great mass of my unbelieving fellow-countrymen either in the highly emotional form offered by revivalists or in the unintelligible language of highly cultured clergymen. Most men were reached by neither. My task was therefore simply that of a *translator*—one turning Christian doctrine, or what he believed to be such, into the vernacular, into language that unscholarly people would attend to and could understand.

Question 6. Why do statements of the Christian faith often seem to take one of two extremes—to paraphrase Lewis, either the highly emotional appeals found at revival meetings or the unintelligible jargon of highly educated theologians? How successful do you think Lewis was in his stated goal: putting Christian doctrine in the language of the common man?

Individual Activity: What I Want to Remember

Complete this activity on your own.

- ◊ Briefly review the readings and any notes you took.
- ◊ In the space below, write down the most significant thing you gained in this session—from your reading, video content, or discussion material.

What I want to remember from this session . . .

Closing Prayer

Close your time together in prayer.

Session 7 Personal Study

Reflect further by exploring additional material from *Mere Christianity* and Scripture.

In the following section of the Nicene Creed we find several of the central tenants of the Christian faith:

> We believe in one Lord, Jesus Christ,
> the only Son of God,
> eternally begotten of the Father,
> God from God, light from light,
> true God from true God,
> begotten, not made,
> of one Being with the Father.

Christian doctrine affirms that Jesus is the Son of God, a position very different from the popular idea of Jesus as merely a great moral teacher with wise advice to help make a better world. Lewis points out that *beget* means to become the father of something of the same kind as yourself. To *make* means to create something of a different kind from yourself. When we affirm that Christ was begotten of the Father, not made, we are saying that he is of the same divine nature as the Father. Lewis concludes, "What God begets is God" (157), and readers may be reminded of the opening words of John 3:16 from the King James Bible, "For God so loved the world, that he gave his only begotten Son ..."

"In a way it is like a human father begetting a human son," Lewis writes. "But not quite like it" (160). One of the main differences is that while a human father and son will be separate beings, the three parts of the Godhead—the Father, Son, and Holy Spirit—remain one being. Lewis highlights another difference two chapters later where he observes that while a human father exists in time before his human son, this is not the case with God and his son.

Question 1. Without the map of theology to guide us, we may feel as though we are free to believe whatever we like about the Christ we experience. Lewis points out that these doctrines of the faith are there to keep us from going off track. For example, in the declaration that Christ was begotten not made, we are reminded that Christ was not simply a good *human* teacher. Can you cite other ways that people may get off track when they neglect or simply do not know Christian doctrine?

If readers are going to understand this concept of one God in three persons—not three separate gods or one God expressed in three different ways—Lewis knows he has to explain. He starts with the idea that most people have: that God has to be more than a person like us, that God is somehow "beyond personality," as the title of Book 4 suggests. Lewis points out the mistake that some people go on to make, which is to then conceive of God as an impersonal being. This, as Lewis notes, makes God less than personal, not more.

Question 2. There are people today who believe in a God but not a personal one. Do you know someone like this? What do you think they mean by a God who is not personal? Where do you think this belief in an impersonal God comes from, and what might you say to them in response?

Question 3. Before Jesus ascended to heaven he said, "Go and make disciples of all nations, baptizing them in the name of the Father and of the Son and of the Holy Spirit" (Matthew 28:19). The doctrine of the Trinity, one God in three persons, is central to the Christian faith. How have you experienced the Father, the Son, and the Holy Spirit in your own life?

Reading Assignment

In preparation for Session 8, read:

- ◊ Book 4, Chapter 9: "Counting the Cost"
- ◊ Book 4, Chapter 10: "Nice People or New Men"

8

Counting the Cost

Reading Assignment

In preparation for Session 8, read:

- ◊ Book 4, Chapter 9: "Counting the Cost"
- ◊ Book 4, Chapter 10: "Nice People or New Men"

Watch Video: *Counting the Cost*

Play the video segment for Session 8. As you watch, take any notes that might be helpful to you in the space provided.

Notes

Video Discussion

Book 4, Chapter 9: Counting the Cost

Lewis opens chapter nine by reporting that a good many people were bothered by what he said in the previous chapter concerning Christ's command to be perfect. Lewis notes that some of them seemed to think that what Jesus was saying was this: "Unless you are perfect, I will not help you" (201). And since none of us can be perfect, our situation is hopeless.

Love God with all your heart, soul, and mind. Love your neighbor as yourself. Take no thought for tomorrow. Do not repay evil with evil. Pray for those who persecute you. When it comes to everyday, real-life decisions, merely being a nice person is not what God is asking of us. "Be perfect" is a far more radical, far more inconvenient command. As Lewis noted in chapter eight, God does not want merely a certain amount of our time or money—he wants *all* of us, every bit. He calls us to be perfect, even though he knows we are flawed. Many people down through the years have heard this radical call and have closed the door on Christianity; they've gone away mumbling that they will never be perfect, so why even try?

But Jesus was *not* telling us that he will not help us unless we are perfect. Instead, as Lewis points out, the command to be perfect means that the only help Christ will give is "help to become perfect" (201). While *we* may want something less than this, he will give us nothing less. Here Lewis tells us that Christ is not like an aspirin we might take to temporarily relieve the pain of a toothache but like a dentist who is going to permanently fix the tooth and all our other teeth as well. A few pages later, Lewis makes a similar comparison: when God comes in to rebuild us, like a builder who is going to fix up an old house, he may start with the drainpipes and the leak in the roof, but he will not stop with anything less than "building a palace" (205). If we will let him, God plans to fix all of our problems—even those problems that we do not particularly want fixed or are unware of.

> **Question 1.** Can you comment on our desire for God to fix just one small aspect in our life and God's intention to make us into entirely new creatures? Lewis notes that our natural tendency is to want God to stop at something less than the "the full treatment" (202). Why do you think this is?

What does this perfect holiness that God insists on look like? In *Heaven, Hell, and Purgatory*, Jerry Walls points out that while we often tend to think of perfection or holiness as "some sort of legalistic demand" that God makes on us, in fact holiness and happiness are inseparably connected, and "the more holy we are, the happier we will be." In this way, Walls concludes, "God's demand of holiness is not some stern, heavy-handed imposition, but rather his passion for our happiness." So for us to aspire to holiness, to be perfectly like Christ, is really to aspire for the only true happiness that is available to us.

Rather than being bad news or discouraging news, Christ's command to be perfect is part of the good news that God has for us, a command made out of love and a critical component of his plan for our ultimate good. In *The Problem of Pain*, Lewis points out, "It is natural for us to wish that God had designed for us a less glorious and less arduous destiny, but then we are wishing not for more love but for less."

Question 2. In the video, Devin Brown points out that Christ's command to be perfect is not a harsh, legalistic demand that sucks all the fun and joy out of life but rather a loving call to the only path that will lead to our happiness. Why do you think so many people have trouble seeing this command as a loving call and not a legalistic ultimatum?

Book 4, Chapter 10: Nice People or New Men

Lewis begins chapter ten by reminding us again that Jesus meant what he said—those people who put themselves in his hands will become perfect, as he is perfect. Lewis then suggests, "The change will not be completed in this life, for death is an important part of the treatment. How far the change will have gone before death in any particular Christian is uncertain" (207).

While at any point we may choose to stop, Lewis points out that if we do not push Christ away, he is going to see the job through. No matter how much suffering it may cost us in our earthly lives or after death, Christ will not rest—and will not let us rest—until we are literally perfect. Here Lewis allows for the possibility of continued growth, the possibility for us to become more Christlike, after death.

Lewis revisits this topic of further perfection after death in *Letters to Malcolm*, where he speculates:

> Would it not break the heart if God said to us, "It is true, my son, that your breath smells and your rags drip with mud and slime, but we are charitable here and no one will upbraid you with these

> things, nor draw away from you. Enter into the joy"? Should we not reply. "With submission, sir, and if there is no objection, I'd *rather* be cleaned first." "It may hurt, you know"—"Even so, sir."
>
> I assume that the process of purification will normally involve suffering. Partly from tradition; partly because most real good that has been done me in this life has involved it. But I don't think suffering is the purpose of the purgation ... The treatment given will be the one required, whether it hurts little or much.

Question 3. In the video, Devin Brown mentions Lewis's point that most Christians are not perfect now nor will be when they die. While this stage need not be called purgatory, does the possibility of our continuing to be made perfect after death, which Lewis raises here, make sense to you? Why or why not? How do you imagine we will ultimately be made perfect?

In the second paragraph of chapter ten, Lewis notes that having fine feelings, or new insights, or a greater interest in "religion" (and he puts this word in quotes to imply that this is an interest not in true religion but in something masquerading as religion)—all these things "mean nothing unless they make our actual behavior better" (207).

Here Lewis visits the age-old problem of people who claim to be Christian but whose behavior suggests the exact opposite, and he is very firm on one point. If becoming a Christian makes no improvement in someone's outward behavior, if they continue to be just as snobbish, spiteful, envious, or ambitious as before their conversion, then—Lewis concludes—we must suspect that their "conversion" (and here again Lewis uses quotes) was "largely imaginary" (207).

Question 4. Lewis reminds us that Jesus himself told us that a tree is known by its fruit (Luke 6:43–45). And when Christians do not behave as Christians should, they make Christianity less credible to the outside world. What would you say to Lewis's claim that, in one sense, the world has a right to judge Christianity by its results—as seen in the lives of those who claim to be Christians?

Lewis now goes on to make the case that while Christians should be expected to be better than they would be without their commitment to Christ, they should not necessarily be expected to be better than all non-believers. For one thing, Lewis points out with great frankness, there are a great many people who are "slowly ceasing to be Christians but who still call themselves by that name" while at the same time there are others who are "slowly becoming Christians though they do not call themselves so" (208).

Here in his discussion of whether Christians are required to become, as the chapter title indicates, nice people or new men (and women), Lewis states his belief on a subject with major implications: that there are people in other religions who are being drawn by God's influence to those parts of their religion which agree with Christianity and so may "belong to Christ without knowing it" (209).

Readers familiar with *The Chronicles of Narnia* know that in *The Last Battle*, Lewis introduces a young man known as Emeth who thought he was following Tash, the demonic god of the Calormenes, but really was following Aslan. As the great lion explains to him, "No service which is vile can be done to me, and none which is not vile can be done to him. Therefore if any man swear by Tash and keep his oath for the oath's sake, it is by me that he has truly sworn, though he know it not, and it is I who reward him."

Question 5. Lewis presents the possibility of people who are slowly becoming Christian but may not realize it and similarly the idea that people from other faiths may belong to Christ without knowing it. What is your position on these topics? Should Christians be expected to be *better* than non-Christians?

Here in chapter ten, Lewis raises the question of whether God calls us to become merely nice people or new men and women. His answer is clearly the latter, and Lewis makes this point fully in the next chapter where he points out that Christ wants not "mere improvement" but transformation (218). Yet this transformation is an odd thing, for, as Lewis writes, "The more we get what we now call 'ourselves' out of the way and let Him take us over, the more truly ourselves we become" (225).

Lewis argues that while the goal is for all Christians to have the mind of Christ and to become more Christlike, God does not take our individuality from us and produce a race of beings who become all exactly the same—quite the opposite.

One of the things Lewis discovered after his conversion was that while, in one sense God wanted to change him entirely, in another sense God had created him in a unique way and valued that uniqueness. In *The Screwtape Letters*, the demon Screwtape explains the seeming paradox this way:

> Of course I know that the Enemy [God] also wants to detach men from themselves, but in a different way. Remember always, that He really likes the little vermin, and sets an absurd value on the distinctness of every one of them. When He talks of their losing their selves, He only means abandoning the clamor of self-will; once they have done that, He really gives them back all their personality, and boasts (I am afraid, sincerely) that when they are wholly His they will be more themselves than ever.

Lewis found that, as he abandoned his self-will, God allowed him to keep his distinct, personal tastes and was more himself than ever.

> **Question 6.** Lewis ends *Mere Christianity* with good news: "Give up yourself and you will find your real self" (226). How have you experienced this finding your real self? What are the voices that urge you to hold on to yourself? What has helped encourage you to give yourself up?

Individual Activity: What I Want to Remember

Complete this activity on your own.

◊ Briefly review the readings and any notes you took.

◊ In the space below, write down the most significant

thing you gained in this session—from your reading, video content, or discussion material.

What I want to remember from this session ...

Closing Prayer

Close your time together in prayer.

Session 8 Personal Study

Reflect further by exploring additional material from *Mere Christianity* and Scripture.

In chapter nine, Lewis reminds readers that Christ warned his followers to count the cost, an allusion to the declaration from Jesus, "Whoever does not bear his own cross and come after me cannot be my disciple. For which of you, desiring to build a tower, does not first sit down and count the cost, whether he has enough to complete it?" (Luke 14:27–28 ESV).

> **Question 1.** If you are already a Christ follower, what did *becoming* his disciple cost you? And what does *being* a Christ follower cost you on a regular basis? If you don't feel the cost is much, why might that be the case?

Lewis continues his focus on God's intention to not merely start our transformation but to complete it, not merely to fix a leaky roof but to rebuild the entire building. The moment we put ourselves in Christ's hands, Lewis reminds us, this is what we are in for—"nothing less, or other" (202). Lewis ended Book 1 of *Mere Christianity* by noting that while Christianity promises unspeakable comfort for those who see it through to the end, it does not begin in comfort. Here we get a sense of the initial discomfort that may be in store for us.

After presenting our monumental call to perfection in the first part of chapter nine, Lewis brings hope and good news in the second half. As Walter Hooper explains in his seminal work, *C. S. Lewis: A Companion Guide*, "Lewis emphasizes that these seemingly impossible demands are put upon us because, with Christ's help, they are possible." We might add that with Christ's help not only is it *possible* for us to become perfect, unless we push him away it is *inevitable.* As Lewis points out, there is no power in the universe, except we ourselves, that can prevent God from taking us to the goal of absolute perfection. God knows that our own efforts are never going to bring us anywhere close to perfection, and every time we fall, he will be there to help us.

Question 2. In an earlier chapter, Lewis asked the question, "Is Christianity hard or easy?" and concluded it was both. Can you expand on this point in connection to Christ's command for us to be perfect?

Question 3. Jesus said, "Be perfect, therefore, as your heavenly Father is perfect" (Matthew 5:48). Lewis writes that the moment we put ourselves in God's hands, this is what we are in for—nothing less or other than being made perfect. How is this both an incredibly terrifying and at the same time an incredibly exciting prospect for you personally?

A LIFE-CHANGING RESPONSE

On Tuesday night, April 4, 1944 at 10:20 pm, C. S. Lewis's final radio broadcast, "The New Man," went out over the airwaves. When told by the BBC's Eric Fenn that the response to the fourth set of talks was sharply divided, either highly favorable or highly critical, Lewis wrote back, "The two views you report (Cat's Whiskers and Beneath Contempt) aren't very illuminating about *me* perhaps; about my subject matter, it is an old story, isn't it? They love, or hate."

For a brief time Lewis considered writing a reply to critics of this final series but quickly decided against it. "I think we'll scrap my 'apologia' altogether on second thought," he told Fenn. "Replies, except in a real rigorous high-brow controversy, are always a mistake."

The end of the broadcast talks did not end Lewis's public career. His output, and the fame that accompanied it, continued to grow—as did the polarized responses to it. On September 8, 1947, Lewis was featured on the cover of *Time* magazine. The writer of the cover story observed, "Outside his own Christian circle, Lewis is not particularly popular with his Oxford colleagues. Some resent his large student following; others criticize his 'cheap' performances on the BBC and sneer at him as a 'popularizer.'" Yet the writer called Lewis "a man who could talk theology without pulling a long face or being dull."

In reality, what Lewis possessed was the extraordinary ability to talk theology without *his audience* pulling a long face. Lewis intended for his audience—if convinced by what he said—to respond in a way that would be life-changing.

In the introduction to the second set of talks, Lewis reminded his listeners that he was going to focus on what all Christians believe, and then added: "In spite of all the unfortunate differences between Christians, what they agree on is still something pretty big and pretty solid: big enough to blow any of us sky-high if it happens to be true."

A 1944 review of the final series of broadcast talks in *The Times Literary Supplement* stated: "Mr. Lewis has a quite unique power of making theology an attractive, exciting and (one might almost say) an uproariously fascinating quest." The reviewer went on to note that, while those who had inherited Christianity might be able to write about it with truth and learning, it took someone like Lewis who had found Christianity after years of unbelief to write about it with the full excitement it deserved.

Lewis's goal in *Mere Christianity* is to take us on a quest for truths that will ultimately not just change how we think but blow us sky-high, to share with us the excitement of someone who had been walking for a long time across a field he was sure was barren and empty—then, to his lifelong wonder and astonishment, discovered a pearl of great price.

Discussing Mere Christianity Study Guide with DVD

Exploring the History, Meaning, and Relevance of C. S. Lewis's Greatest Book

Devin Brown and Eric Metaxas

In this 8-session video group study, you will discover why *Mere Christianity* by C. S. Lewis is one of the most read and beloved Christian books of all time. But seventy years after it was first delivered on radio, what relevance does it have to our world today? Host Eric Metaxas and a variety of Christian leaders (including Philip Yancey, Alister McGrath, Devin Brown, Paul McCusker, and Douglas Gresham) help us understand the timeless message of C. S. Lewis in fresh ways for a new generation.

The first purpose of this video study is to explore the positive ideas that C. S. Lewis has so eloquently written about in *Mere Christianity* for those who already call themselves Christian. The second purpose is to explain in an engaging, winsome, and non-threatening way the basic tenets of the Christian faith as illustrated by C. S. Lewis to those who do not claim to be Christian. This study aims to fulfill the vision of C. S. Lewis of reaching people from all faith backgrounds.

This pack contains one softcover study guide and one DVD in Amaray case.

Available in stores and online!